J978.9
H

New Mexico

BY ANN HEINRICHS

Content Adviser: Guadalupe A. Martinez, Southwest Collections, New Mexico State Library, Santa Fe, New Mexico

Reading Adviser: Dr. Linda D. Labbo, Department of Reading Education, College of Education, The University of Georgia

COMPASS POINT BOOKS MINNEAPOLIS, MINNESOTA

Compass Point Books
3109 West 50th Street, #115
Minneapolis, MN 55410

Visit Compass Point Books on the Internet at *www.compasspointbooks.com*
or e-mail your request to *custserv@compasspointbooks.com*

On the cover: Homes built into the cliffs of Chaco Canyon by the ancient Pueblo people

Photographs ©: Digital Stock, cover, 1, 3, 34; N.Carter/North Wind Picture Archives, 5, 13, 26, 32;
John Elk III, 7, 8, 10, 17, 27, 29, 31, 33, 36, 40, 41, 42, 43 (top), 45, 47, 48 (top); Photo Network/Bill
Terry, 9; KAC Productions/Greg Lasley, 11; Mark & Sue Werner/The Image Finders, 12; Unicorn Stock
Photos/Ernesto Burciaga, 14; North Wind Picture Archives, 15, 16, 18; Hulton/Archive by Getty Images,
19; Getty Images, 20, 28, 46; Photo Network/Margo Taussig Pinkerton, 21; Unicorn Stock Photos/
Andre Jenny, 22; James P. Rowan, 24; Unicorn Stock Photos/Deneve Feigh Bunde, 25; Photo Network/
Mark Newman, 30; Unicorn Stock Photos/Mark E. Gibson, 37; Unicorn Stock Photos/Ann Trulove, 38;
Robesus, Inc., 43 (state flag); One Mile Up, Inc., 43 (state seal); Joe McDonald/Visuals Unlimited, 44
(top); A.J. Copley/Visuals Unlimited, 44 (middle); Comstock, 44 (bottom).

Editors: E. Russell Primm, Emily J. Dolbear, and Catherine Neitge
Photo Researcher: Marcie C. Spence
Photo Selector: Linda S. Koutris
Designer/Page Production: The Design Lab/Jaime Martens
Cartographer: XNR Productions, Inc.

Library of Congress Cataloging-in-Publication Data
Heinrichs, Ann.
  New Mexico / by Ann Heinrichs.
     p. cm. — (This land is your land)
  Summary: Describes the geography, history, government, people, culture, and attractions of New
Mexico. Includes bibliographical references (p.) and index.
    ISBN 0-7565-0343-4 (hardcover : alk. paper)
  1. New Mexico—Juvenile literature. [1. New Mexico.] I. Title.
    F796.3 .H45 2004
    978.9—dc21   2002151672

Table of Contents

NOTE: In this book, words that are defined in the glossary are in **bold** the first time they appear in the text.

Welcome to New Mexico!

William Blake traveled through New Mexico in the 1850s. Near the town of Zuni, he saw a fantastic sight. It was a towering mesa—a high, flat-topped hill. Blake was amazed by the mesa's rocky slopes. He wrote: "These banks have been worn into many fantastic shapes by the action of the weather for ages." He said they "seem to be the work of art."

Sights like this still amaze visitors today. New Mexico is famous for its rugged beauty. It is a land of high mountains, deep canyons, broad deserts, and strange rock formations.

Native Americans have lived in New Mexico since ancient times. **Hispanic** people have lived there for hundreds of years. Both **cultures** are very much a part of New Mexican life today.

In spite of its ancient history, New Mexico is quite modern. Many scientists work in the state's **research** centers. Their discoveries opened up the space age and **nuclear energy.** Now explore New Mexico—and make discoveries of your own!

▲ This rock formation is along the Acoma-Zuni Trail.

Mountains, Deserts, and Canyons

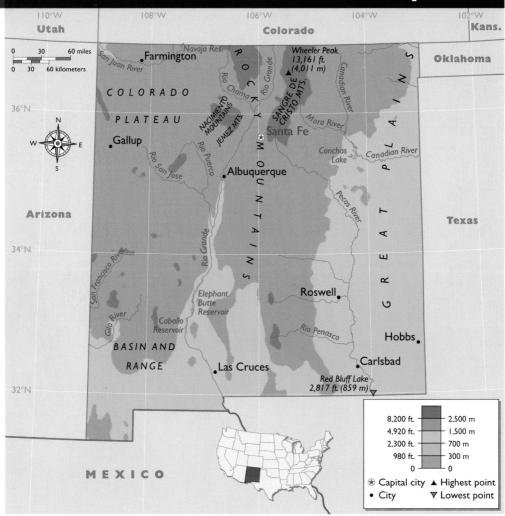

Farmington
Navajo Res.
Wheeler Peak
13,161 ft.
(4,011 m)
San Juan River
ROCKY
Rio Chama
Rio Grande
SANGRE DE CRISTO MTS.
COLORADO
NACIMIENTO MOUNTAINS
Mora River
PLATEAU
JEMEZ MTS.
Santa Fe
Canadian River
Gallup
Conchas Lake
Canadian River
Rio San Jose
Rio Puerco
Rio Grande
Albuquerque
MOUNTAINS
Pecos River
GREAT PLAINS
San Francisco River
Roswell
Elephant Butte Reservoir
Gila River
Caballo Reservoir
Rio Penasco
Hobbs
BASIN AND
RANGE
Las Cruces
Carlsbad
Red Bluff Lake
2,817 ft (859 m)

Utah
110°W · 108°W · 106°W · 104°W · 102°W
Colorado
Kans.
Oklahoma
36°N
Arizona
Texas
34°N
32°N
MEXICO

8,200 ft.	2,500 m
4,920 ft.	1,500 m
2,300 ft.	700 m
980 ft.	300 m
0	0

⊛ Capital city ▲ Highest point
• City ▼ Lowest point

0 30 60 miles
0 30 60 kilometers

N W E S

▲ **A topographic map of New Mexico**

New Mexico is one of America's southwestern states, and it's big! It is the country's fifth-largest state in area. To the south is Texas and the country of Mexico. Texas and a small part of Oklahoma lie to

▲ The Jemez Canyon is located in the Jemez Mountains in New Mexico's Rockies.

the east. To the north is Colorado, and to the west is Arizona. A corner of Utah touches northwest New Mexico.

New Mexico's northwest corner is part of the Four Corners area. New Mexico, Colorado, Utah, and Arizona all meet there. They form a perfect four-corner angle. It's the only place in the United States where four states meet at one point.

New Mexico is a land of deserts, high mountains, and deep canyons. North-central New Mexico is part of the Rocky Mountains, or Rockies. These rugged mountains reach into the state from Colorado. The Sangre de Cristo, Nacimiento, and Jemez mountain ranges are all part of New Mexico's Rockies.

Santa Fe, the state capital, lies high in this mountainous region.

Northwestern New Mexico is on the Colorado Plateau. It has many valleys, rocky cliffs, and canyons. High mesas rise above the plains. The word *mesa* is Spanish for "table."

The Basin and Range region covers southwestern New Mexico. Its basins are broad stretches of low-lying desert. Many mountain ranges rise over them. White Sands National Monument is a glistening white desert. Its "sands" are not regular sand, but a mineral called gypsum.

▲ A visitor walks on the gypsum at White Sands National Monument.

▲ **The Rio Grande is New Mexico's major river.**

Eastern New Mexico is part of the country's Great Plains. Many cattle and sheep ranches stretch across this region. In some places, rivers and streams have carved out deep canyons.

New Mexico's major river is the Rio Grande. (*Rio Grande* is Spanish for "big river.") The river begins in Colorado's Rocky Mountains. It runs all the way down the center of New Mexico.

▲ Albuquerque is New Mexico's largest city.

The fertile Rio Grande Valley is one of New Mexico's best farming regions. Albuquerque, the state's largest city, developed beside the Rio Grande. Farther south, a dam on the river creates Elephant Butte Reservoir. This is New Mexico's largest lake.

The Pecos River runs through the southeastern plains. The Canadian River is the major river in the northeast. The San Juan River is the main river in the northwest. **Irrigation** brings water from the rivers to much of the state's farmland.

▲ **Spring along the Pecos River**

▲ **New Mexico is home to mountain lions.**

Forests cover the mountainsides and high mountain valleys. They shelter bears, deer, and mountain lions. Among the smaller animals are chipmunks, foxes, and bobcats. Prairie dogs, coyotes, and jackrabbits scamper across the deserts and plains. You probably know a different name for the chaparral, the state bird. It's also called the roadrunner.

Some of the desert's hardy plants are cactus, mesquite, creosote, and sage. The yucca, the state flower, grows almost everywhere in New Mexico. The piñon pine is the state tree. People have eaten its seeds, called piñon nuts, for hundreds of years.

New Mexico's weather is warm and dry. Many people retire in New Mexico because of its climate. Sudden thunderstorms sometimes sweep through in the summer. They end quickly, leaving the air dry again. The western part of the

▲ The cholla cactus grows in New Mexico's Gila National Forest.

▲ **Winter in the Jemez Mountains**

state gets the least rainfall. Heavy snows blanket the northern

mountains in the winter. In the spring, melting snow swells

the Rio Grande and other rivers.

A Trip Through Time

Almost two thousand years ago, the ancient Pueblo people lived in New Mexico. They made their homes in the Four Corners area. Some lived in cliff caves or on the mesa tops. Others built stone **pueblos,** or group housing. Some pueblos stood several stories high. The ancient Puebloans grew maize (corn), pumpkins, beans, and cotton. They held religious ceremonies in kivas, or round rooms that are partially underground. They were the ancestors of today's Pueblo Indians.

▲ An ancient Pueblo woman carrying water up a mesa in a clay pot

The Mogollon people lived in the Southwest. They gathered roots and nuts and made pottery. Their houses were in pits they dug into the ground. In the 1400s, Navajo and Apache people came to New Mexico from the north.

Spanish explorers from Mexico were the first Europeans in New Mexico. At that time, Mexico was a Spanish colony. Francisco Vásquez de Coronado passed through in 1540. He was looking for cities of gold, but he did not find any. In 1598, Juan de Oñate set up a Spanish colony in northern New Mexico. He named it the Pueblo of San Juan de los Caballeros. Santa Fe became the colony's capital in 1610.

▲ **Pueblo Indians participating in a ceremonial dance during the 1800s**

▲ Remains of the Mission San Gregorio de Abo in the Salinas Pueblo National Monument

Spanish settlers forced the Pueblo Indians to work on their farms. Spanish priests built Roman Catholic missions. They tried to convert the Native Americans to Christianity. Unhappy with their Spanish rulers, the Native Americans fought them in the Pueblo Revolt of 1680. They drove out the Spaniards and their religion, but only for a short time. More Spaniards soon settled throughout New Mexico.

Mexico won its independence from Spain in 1821. Then New Mexico became a colony of the Republic of Mexico. Meanwhile, American farmers and trappers were pushing into the region. During the Mexican War (1846–1848), U.S. troops invaded Mexico and gained most of New Mexico and much of today's western United States.

▲ In 1846, General Stephen Watts Kearny marched his troops into New Mexico and declared it an American territory.

New Mexico Territory was created in 1850. Thousands of settlers arrived in covered wagons along the Santa Fe Trail. This route stretched from Independence, Missouri, to Santa Fe.

Huge ranches spread across New Mexico. Cowboys went on cattle drives to herd the cattle to market centers. Cattle and sheep ranchers often fought each other for land rights. Conflicts also broke out between small-scale farmers and big landowners.

Little by little, American Indian groups were driven out or sent to **reservations.** The Navajo retreated to a reservation in New Mexico Territory in 1868. Apaches resisted American troops until 1886, when they also moved onto a reservation. In the 1880s, railroads brought in a flood of new settlers.

New Mexico became the forty-seventh U.S. state in 1912. The state suffered a serious drought, or lack of rain, in the 1920s. Many farmers and ranchers lost their crops and herds. However, oil and other minerals were discovered around the same time.

▲ **The Santa Fe Railroad brought many new settlers to New Mexico.**

In the 1940s, the U.S. government opened a secret research center at Los Alamos. Scientists there developed an atomic bomb. To test the bomb, they exploded it near Alamogordo in July 1945. A month later, the U.S. dropped atomic bombs on Japan and ended World War II (1939–1945).

After the war, the government expanded its activities in New Mexico. Both Los Alamos and Albuquerque became large research centers. Hundreds of scientists and engineers moved into the state. Tourism grew as more and more people

▲ **The atomic bomb was first tested near Alamogordo in 1945.**

▲ Visitors explore an ancient Pueblo cliff dwelling in Bandelier National Monument.

discovered New Mexico. Today, both government work and tourism are big industries. Some visitors come to explore New Mexico's historic sites. Others simply enjoy the beauty of its natural areas.

Government by the People

▲ The state capitol in Santa Fe

In New Mexico, even children get involved in their government. Elementary school students in Edgewood were studying the United States. They found that many states had a state insect, but not New Mexico. So they took matters into their own hands. They mailed voting forms to students throughout the state. When the votes came in, the tarantula hawk wasp won. The Edgewood students urged their state lawmakers to make it the state insect—and they did!

Americans take part in their government in many ways. One important way is to vote for their government officials. Those officials serve in three branches of government—legislative, executive, and judicial. Both the U.S. government and New Mexico's state government are organized this way.

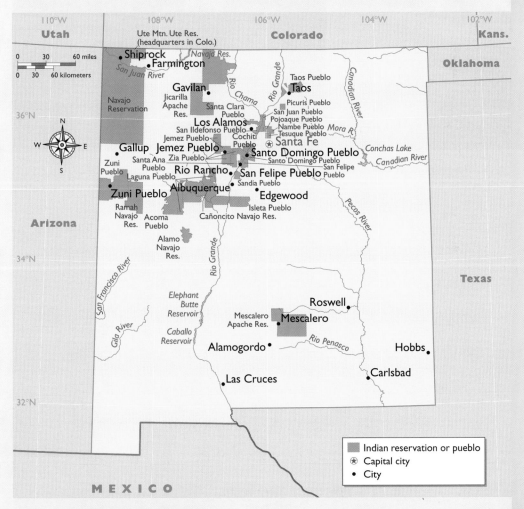

▲ **A geopolitical map of New Mexico**

▲ **The Eddy County Courthouse in Carlsbad**

New Mexico's legislative branch makes the state laws. Voters choose their lawmakers to serve in the state legislature. It's divided into two houses, or parts. One is the forty-two-member senate. The other is the seventy-member house of representatives. They all meet in the state capitol in Santa Fe.

The governor is the head of the executive branch. This branch makes sure that people obey the laws. Voters elect the governor and many other executive officers to a four-year term. Each officer may serve only two terms in a row.

Judges and their courts make up the judicial branch. The judges study the laws and decide if they have been broken. Voters elect their judges. New Mexico's five-member supreme court is the state's highest court.

New Mexico is divided into thirty-three counties. Los Alamos County is governed by a city-county council. In all the other counties, voters elect a board of commissioners. Cities, towns, and villages have various forms of government. Most elect mayors or managers and councils or commissions.

New Mexico has six Native American reservations. Each one has a tribal government system. In this system, each reservation is governed by tribal leaders, councils, and laws. In some cases, tribal law is followed instead of state law.

▲ **The Institute of American Indian Arts Museum is in Santa Fe.**

People were farming in present-day New Mexico as early as six thousand years ago. Long before Europeans arrived, Native Americans were using irrigation. They dug canals to bring water from the rivers to their fields.

In the 1800s, most New Mexicans were farmers or ranchers. Then mining, manufacturing, and other industries opened up new types of jobs. Farming and ranching are still important to New Mexico, though. Farmland covers more than half the state. Most of that land is grazing land for cattle ranches.

Beef cattle are New Mexico's top agricultural product. Next in value is milk. Many ranchers raise dairy cattle, sheep, and hogs. Irrigation brings water to most of the state's croplands. New Mexico leads the nation in producing chiles, or hot peppers. Farmers

▲ This Texas longhorn is grazing on a ranch near the southern Gila Mountains.

▲ **Molybdenum, used for making steel, is mined in Questa.**

also grow hay, onions, peanuts, pecans, cotton, and wheat. Decorative trees and flowers are important products, too.

New Mexico has many valuable minerals. Petroleum (oil) and natural gas are the state's top mining products. Pipelines carry much of the natural gas to other states. Copper, potash, coal, molybdenum, and uranium are also mined. Potash is made into fertilizer, and molybdenum is used for making steel.

New Mexico's leading factory goods are computers and other electronics. Two computer giants—Intel and Honeywell—have factories near Albuquerque. Other factories make chemicals, foods, clothes, and petroleum products.

More than four out of five New Mexico workers hold service jobs. Service workers sell their helpful skills instead of products. Some work in hospitals, restaurants, or tourist areas. Others may drive trucks, sell houses, or repair equipment.

One part of the service industry is government work. About one out of five workers in the state has a government job. Many work at Sandia National Laboratories in Albuquerque or Los Alamos National Laboratory. Both are centers for research on nuclear energy. New Mexico has many military bases, too. They include White Sands Missile Range and three air force bases.

▲ An Air Force jet fires a missile during a training mission over the desert of White Sands Missile Range.

▲ People enjoying a pretty day in the central plaza of Santa Fe

New Mexico is one of America's fastest-growing states. In 2000, the state had 1,819,046 residents. That's almost three times as large as its population in 1950! Still, there is plenty of room to go around. Remember—in land area, New Mexico is the fifth-largest state, but it only ranks thirty-sixth in population.

Many parts of New Mexico are very thinly settled. Most people live around big cities and along the river valleys. Albuquerque, on the Rio Grande, is the state's largest city. More than one out of three New Mexicans lives in or around Albuquerque. Next in size are Las Cruces and Santa Fe.

▲ **Zuni Tewa dancers perform at the Indian Pueblo Cultural Center in Albuquerque.**

People of three major cultures live in New Mexico. They are Native Americans, Hispanics, and Anglo-Americans. Many people are mixtures of these three.

More than two out of five people are Hispanic. Some descended from the state's early Spanish and Mexican settlers. Others arrived more recently. About two out of three New Mexicans are Anglo-Americans. They are descendants of Europeans. This group includes many Hispanics, who may be of any race.

Almost one out of ten New Mexicans is Native American. The major groups are the Navajo, Pueblo, and Apache. They live in six reservations and nineteen pueblos, or towns. The word *pueblo* also refers to the town's community houses. They are made of adobe, or sun-dried mud bricks. The state's largest group is the Navajo. Their reservation is in northwestern New Mexico.

New Mexico's many cultures come alive in colorful festivals. Native Americans hold ceremonies throughout the state. Many include traditional dances. San Felipe and Santo Domingo Pueblos hold the Green Corn Dance. The Sun Dance is performed at Taos Pueblo's Fiesta of San Geronimo. Performers present the Harvest Dance at Jemez Pueblo's Fiesta of San Diego. Apaches hold a ceremonial in Mescalero, and Zuni Pueblo hosts the Shalako Ceremonial. Dozens of American Indian groups attend the International Ceremonial in Gallup.

The Santa Fe Fiesta is New Mexico's largest Hispanic festival. It begins with the burning of Zozobra, a gigantic puppet. His name means "old man gloom."

▲ A young Native American dancer at a festival in San Juan Pueblo

He is a symbol of the past year's hardships. As the puppet
burns, dancers perform and the crowds cheer. Many other
towns and villages have similar fiestas.

Many cowboys work on New Mexico's ranches. They also
take part in rodeos all over the state. The Whole Enchilada
Fiesta is a three-day festival in Las Cruces. The festival's
cooks make the world's largest enchilada. That's a corn tor-
tilla, or flat bread, spread with meat or cheese and covered

▲ **A rodeo in Gallup**

with red or green chile sauce. Albuquerque hosts the International Hot Air Balloon Festival every October. Hundreds of brightly colored balloons float across the sky.

Artists love to paint scenes of New Mexico. Artist Georgia O'Keeffe lived in New Mexico for many years. She painted huge pictures of animal bones, deserts, flowers, and other scenes from nature she saw there. Today, large communities of artists live in Taos, Santa Fe, and Albuquerque.

▲ This handcrafted kachina doll represents a figure in the spirit world.

Native Americans have had their own arts for hundreds of years. They make beautiful pottery, blankets, baskets, and jewelry. The Hopi and Zuni make kachinas, or dolls that represent spirits.

Hispanic artists make pottery, woven cloth, and objects carved from wood or bone. Some make *bultos,* or sculptures of religious figures.

▲ The ancient Pueblo people built these homes into the cliffs of Chaco Canyon.

New Mexico preserves many ruins from ancient Native American cultures. Near Albuquerque is Petroglyph National Monument. Thousands of petroglyphs, or rock pictures, are carved into the rocks there. A four-hundred-room pueblo of the ancient Pueblo people makes up the Aztec Ruins. Chaco Canyon contains many ancient Pueblo communities. Other prehistoric ruins are the Gila and Puye cliff dwellings and Bandelier National Monument.

El Rancho de las Golondrinas is south of Santa Fe. Its name

means "the ranch of the swallows." It was an important stop along the *Camino Real,* or Royal Road, between Santa Fe and Mexico City, Mexico. Today, its villagers dress in a style of clothing from the 1700s. They show how people lived and worked in Spanish colonial days.

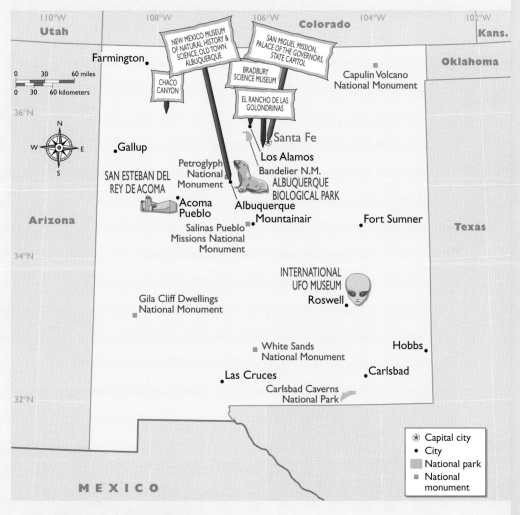

▲ **Places to visit in New Mexico**

New Mexico's many Spanish missions give another glimpse into those times. Several churches still stand at the Salinas Pueblo Missions in Mountainair. San Esteban del Rey de Acoma is at Acoma Pueblo near Albuquerque. It was founded in 1629 and is still in use. San Miguel Mission is in Santa Fe. Spaniards built it during the 1600s.

Santa Fe, the capital city, is perched high in the northern mountains. Spaniards built the Palace of the Governors there in 1610. Today, it's a southwestern history museum. It's the country's oldest public building that's still being used. The modern state capitol is built in the shape of a *Zia*. This is an ancient Native American symbol for the sun.

▲ **The Mission of San Miguel in Santa Fe**

▲ **Visitors learn about conservation at the Albuquerque Biological Park.**

Sandia Peak near Albuquerque is a popular ski area, but you don't have to be a skier to ride the tramway. This overhead ride is the world's longest tramway. Back down on the ground, be sure to visit Albuquerque Biological Park. It includes a zoo, aquarium, and gardens. You can ride a horse-drawn carriage through Old Town Albuquerque. You'll pass village shops with Spanish, Native American, and Anglo crafts and foods.

▲ Visitors preparing to enter the New Mexico Museum of Natural History and Science in Albuquerque

Travel back in time at Albuquerque's New Mexico Museum of Natural History and Science. Several of its exhibits explore the dinosaur age. For even more science, visit the Bradbury Science Museum at Los Alamos. There you'll find out how nuclear energy developed. You'll also learn about the latest in lasers, computers, solar energy, and much more. The Space Hall of Fame is in Alamogordo. Many rockets and spacecraft show the development of space flight.

Are you a UFO fan? (UFOs are unidentified flying objects.) Then you won't want to miss Roswell! Some people believe that an alien spacecraft crashed there in 1947. You can learn all about aliens at Roswell's International UFO Museum. Also in eastern New Mexico is the small village of Fort Sumner. Here you can visit the grave of legendary outlaw Billy the Kid.

New Mexico is rich in natural wonders. Strangely shaped rock formations are scattered throughout the state. Glistening white dunes stretch across White Sands National Monument. Weird rock formations called hoodoos are created by the weather in the Bisti Badlands National Monument near the Navajo reservation. Towering red rocks rise over deserts and plains. Shiprock, in the northwest, is shaped like a tall sailing ship.

Capulin Mountain is actually the remains of an ancient volcano. Red-hot lava would flow for miles when it erupted. The cooled-off lava formed a hill that is now called Capulin.

▲ **Carlsbad Caverns contains many interesting rock formations.**

Carlsbad Caverns is in southeastern New Mexico. It's a massive network of gigantic caves with amazing rock formations. The caves are also home to a huge colony of bats.

As you can see, from its amazing landscape to its colorful history, New Mexico is a great place to explore!

Important Dates

1540 Francisco Vásquez de Coronado explores present-day New Mexico.

1598 Juan de Oñate establishes San Juan, New Mexico's first permanent Spanish colony.

1680 Pueblo Indians in northern New Mexico revolt against the Spanish there.

1821 Mexico wins independence from Spain; New Mexico becomes a colony of Mexico.

1848 The Mexican War ends, and New Mexico becomes part of the United States.

1850 New Mexico Territory is established.

1886 The Apache Wars end with the surrender of Geronimo.

1912 New Mexico becomes the forty-seventh state on January 6.

1922 Oil is discovered in New Mexico.

1945 The world's first atomic bomb is exploded near Alamogordo.

1950 Uranium is discovered in northwestern New Mexico.

1970s The San Juan–Chama project brings water to north-central New Mexico.

1982 The U.S. Supreme Court rules that American Indian nations may charge taxes on minerals mined from their lands.

1998 New Mexicans celebrate the 400th anniversary of the San Juan colony.

Glossary

cultures—groups of people who share beliefs, customs, and a way of life

Hispanic—people of Mexican, South American, and other Spanish-speaking cultures

irrigation—a way of bringing water to fields through canals, or ditches

missions—settlements made to spread religious teachings

nuclear energy—energy created by splitting tiny particles of matter

pueblos—buildings where many families live; Native American towns

research—scientific study

reservations—large areas of land set aside for Native Americans

Did You Know?

★ Santa Fe is the highest state capital in America. It's about 7,000 feet (2,134 meters) above sea level.

★ Leaves of the yucca plant can be made into rope, baskets, and sandals.

★ In 1950, a little bear cub was rescued from a tree in New Mexico during a forest fire. Rescuers named the cub Smokey. He became the symbol of the national fire safety campaign. Until that time, there was a cartoon version of Smokey Bear.

★ The Navajo are the nation's largest American Indian group.

★ Santa Fe is the second-oldest city settled by Europeans in the United States. Only Saint Augustine, Florida, is older.

★ Taos Pueblo, about 3 miles (4.8 kilometers) north of the town of Taos, is about six hundred years old.

★ Only Alaska, Texas, California, and Montana are larger in size than New Mexico.

At a Glance

State capital: Santa Fe

State motto: *Crescit Eundo* (Latin for "it grows as it goes")

State nickname: Land of Enchantment

Statehood: January 6, 1912; forty-seventh state

Land area: 121,365 square miles (314,335 sq km); **rank:** fifth

Highest point: Wheeler Peak, 13,161 feet (4,011 m)

Lowest point: Red Bluff Reservoir in Eddy County, 2,817 feet (859 m) above sea level

Highest recorded temperature: 122°F (50°C) at Waste Isolation Pilot Plant near Carlsbad on June 27, 1994

Lowest recorded temperature: −50°F (−46°C) at Gavilan on February 1, 1951

Average January temperature: 34°F (1°C)

Average July temperature: 74°F (23°C)

Population in 2000: 1,819,046; **rank:** thirty-sixth

Largest cities in 2000: Albuquerque (448,607), Las Cruces (74,267), Santa Fe (62,203), Rio Rancho (51,765)

Factory products: Electrical equipment, scientific instruments, foods

Farm products: Beef cattle, milk, hay

Mining products: Natural gas, petroleum, copper

State flag: New Mexico's state flag features a red *Zia,* an ancient Native American symbol for the sun. Its sixteen rays stand for

important times and events in the natural world. Four rays stand for the four directions: north, south, east, and west. Four stand for the four seasons: winter, spring, summer, and fall. Four represent the times of day: dawn, daylight, dusk, and dark. And four stand for the four stages of human life: infancy, youth, adulthood, and old age. The *Zia* stands against a field of gold.

State seal: The state seal shows two eagles. The larger one is an American bald eagle. It stands for bravery, skill, and strength. This eagle is grasping three arrows in its claws. The bald eagle is spreading its wings to protect the smaller Mexican eagle. That eagle holds a snake in its beak and a cactus in its claws. This set of symbols is the official symbol of Mexico. It's based on an Aztec myth. According to this myth, the gods told the Aztecs to settle where they saw an eagle perched on a cactus with a snake in its beak. Beneath the eagles is a banner with the state motto.

State abbreviations: N. Mex. or N.M. (traditional); NM (postal)

State Symbols

State bird: Chaparral (roadrunner)

State flower: Yucca

State tree: Piñon

State grass: Blue grama

State animal: Black bear

State fish: Cutthroat trout

State vegetables: Chile and *frijole* (beans)

State insect: Tarantula hawk wasp

State gem: Turquoise

State cookie: Biscochito

State fossil: *Coelophysis*

Making Biscochitos

Biscochitos are New Mexico's state cookie.

Makes about fifty cookies.

INGREDIENTS:

2 ½ cups shortening

1 ½ cups sugar

2 eggs

2 teaspoons crushed anise seed

6 cups flour

3 teaspoons baking powder

1 teaspoon salt

½ cup fruit juice

3 teaspoons cinnamon

1 cup sugar

DIRECTIONS:

Make sure an adult helps you with the hot stove. Preheat the oven to 350°F. Put the shortening in a mixing bowl. Slowly beat in the sugar. Add the eggs one by one, and beat until it's fluffy. Mix in the anise seed. In another bowl, mix the flour, baking powder, and salt. Slowly mix this into the wet mixture. Add the juice. Let this mixture stand for about 10 minutes. Then put the dough on a floured board and roll it out. Cut into 2-inch squares and place them on an ungreased cookie sheet. Bake for 10 to 15 minutes. While they're baking, mix together the cinnamon and sugar. Sprinkle it on top of the cookies as soon as they come out of the oven.

"O, Fair New Mexico"

Words and music by Elizabeth Garrett, daughter of Pat Garrett, the legendary sheriff who killed Billy the Kid

Under a sky of azure, where balmy breezes blow,
Kissed by the golden sunshine, is Nuevo Mejico.
Land of the Montezuma, with fiery hearts aglow,
Land of the deeds historic, is Nuevo Mejico.

Chorus:
Oh! Fair New Mexico, we love, we love you so,
Our hearts with pride o'erflow,
No matter where we go.
Oh! Fair New Mexico, we love, we love you so,
The grandest state we know—New Mexico!

Rugged and high sierras, with deep canyons below,
Dotted with fertile valleys, is Nuevo Mejico.
Fields full of sweet alfalfa, richest perfumes bestow,
State of apple blossoms, is Nuevo Mejico.

Days that are full of heart-dreams, nights when the moon hangs low;
Beaming its benedictions, o'er Nuevo Mejico.
Land with its bright mañana, coming through weal and woe;
State of esperanza, is Nuevo Mejico.

Robert Goddard (1882–1945) was a scientist who developed rockets and other spacecraft. He is called the father of modern rocketry. Goddard was born in Massachusetts but did much of his work in Roswell.

Sid Gutierrez (1951–) is an astronaut. He performed missions on Spacelab and the space shuttle *Endeavour.* He was born in Albuquerque.

William Hanna (1910–2001) was a cartoonist who worked with Joseph Barbera. They created the animated characters Yogi Bear, Scooby-Doo, and Tom and Jerry. He was born in Melrose.

Tony Hillerman (1925–) has written many award-winning mysteries. Most of his novels are set in western New Mexico and feature two Navajo police officers. Hillerman grew up in Oklahoma and moved to New Mexico in the early 1950s.

Conrad Hilton (1887–1979) founded Hilton Hotels, one of the world's largest hotel chains. He was born in the small town of San Antonio.

Nancy Lopez (1957–) is a professional golfer. She has won the LPGA championship three times. She was born in California and grew up in Roswell, where an elementary school has been named for her.

Bill Mauldin (1921-2003) was a cartoonist who made fun of political figures and events. He won the first of his two Pulitzer Prizes for his World War II cartoons featuring young soldiers Willie and Joe. He was born near Santa Fe.

Henry McCarty (1859–1881) was the real name of the legendary outlaw Billy the Kid. The young gunman has been portrayed in many books and movies. He was born in New York and moved to New Mexico as a young man. He was shot and killed in Fort Sumner by Sheriff Pat Garrett.

Demi Moore (1962–) is an actress. Her movies include *Ghost* (1990) and *G.I. Jane* (1997). Moore (pictured above left) was born Demi Guynes in Roswell.

Georgia O'Keeffe (1887–1986) was an artist who painted huge pictures of flowers, desert scenes, and animal bones. She was born in Wisconsin and later moved to New Mexico.

Popé (1630–1692) led the Pueblo Revolt of 1680. After the Spaniards were driven out, he worked to restore Pueblo culture.

Al Unser Sr. (1939–) is a race car driver. He has won the Indianapolis 500 four times. His brother, **Bobby Unser** (1934–) has won the Indy 500 three times. Al's son, **Al Unser Jr.** (1962–) has won the Indy 500 twice. The Albuquerque race car drivers have also won many other races.

Victorio (1825–1880) was a Mimbreño Apache chief. He led his people in fighting to regain their lands in the Black Mountains.

Want to Know More?

At the Library

De Angelis, Therese. *New Mexico.* Danbury, Conn.: Children's Press, 2002.

Hillerman, Tony, and Janet Grado (illustrator). *The Boy Who Made Dragonfly: A Zuni Myth.* Albuquerque: University of New Mexico Press, 1999.

Joseph, Paul. *New Mexico.* Edina, Minn.: Abdo & Daughters, 1998.

Kavasch, E. Barrie. *Apache Children and Elders Talk Together.* New York: PowerKids Press, 1999.

Morris, John Miller. *From Coronado to Escalante.* New York: Chelsea House, 1992.

Peña, Abe M. *Memories of Cibola: Stories from New Mexico Villages.* Albuquerque: University of New Mexico Press, 1997.

On the Web

Welcome to New Mexico
http://www.state.nm.us/
To visit New Mexico's state government web site

New Mexico Department of Tourism
http://www.newmexico.org
To find out about New Mexico's events, activities, and sights

Through the Mail

New Mexico Department of Tourism
491 Old Santa Fe Trail
Santa Fe, NM 87503
For information on travel and interesting sights in New Mexico

Historical Society of New Mexico
P.O. Box 1912
Santa Fe, NM 87504
For information on New Mexico's history

Legislative Council Service
Room 411, State Capitol
Santa Fe, NM 87501
For information on New Mexico's state government

On the Road

New Mexico State Capitol
Paseo de Peralta and Old Santa Fe Trail
Santa Fe, NM 87501
505/827-3000
To visit New Mexico's state capitol

Index

About the Author

Ann Heinrichs grew up in Fort Smith, Arkansas, and lives in Chicago. She is the author of more than one hundred books for children and young adults on Asian, African, and U.S. history and culture. Ann has also written numerous newspaper, magazine, and encyclopedia articles. She is an award-winning martial artist, specializing in t'ai chi empty-hand and sword forms.

Ann has traveled widely throughout the United States, Africa, Asia, and the Middle East. In exploring each state for this series, she rediscovered the people, history, and resources that make this a great land, as well as the concerns we share with people around the world.